Stranger than Fiction: Urban Myths

PHIL HEALEY and RICK GLANVILL

Level 2

Retold by Patty Key and Stephen Kirby
Series Editors: Andy Hopkins and Jocelyn Potter

T3-BHM-493

Pearson Education Limited
Edinburgh Gate, Harlow,
Essex CM20 2JE, England
and Associated Companies throughout the world.

ISBN 0 582 41791 0

First published in Great Britain by Virgin Books 1992
This adaptation first published by Penguin Books 1998
Published by Addison Wesley Longman Limited and Penguin Books Ltd. 1998
New edition first published 1999
Third impression 2001
Original copyright © Phil Healey and Rick Glanville 1992
Text copyright © Patty Key and Stephen Kirby 1998
Illustrations copyright © Clive Collins 1998
All rights reserved

Typeset by Digital Type, London
Set in 11/14pt Bembo
Printed in Spain by Mateu Cromo, S. A. Pinto (Madrid)

Published by Pearson Education Limited in association with
Penguin Books Ltd, both companies being subsidiaries of Pearson Plc

For a complete list of the titles available in the Penguin Readers series please write to your local
Pearson Education office or to: Marketing Department, Penguin Longman Publishing,
5 Bentinck Street, London W1M 5RN.

Contents

Introduction

One afternoon a famous television news-reader drove very fast in his open-topped car along a big road. Suddenly there was a strange noise . . . THUD! 'What's that?' he thought. He stopped, turned round and looked – there was a cow in the back! It was dead.

In the world today interesting and strange things often happen. Sometimes it is something happy, sometimes something sad. Sometimes people want to laugh about it, sometimes they want to cry.

In this book there are different stories about some of these strange and interesting things. What happened to the man when he fell from the Empire State Building in New York? Who was the old woman at the bus-stop with hair on her hands? What fell out of the old man's ear, and why did everybody laugh? Can cows fly?

This book will answer these interesting questions for you. And who knows? Perhaps something as strange as this will happen to you . . .?

Phil Healey and Rick Glanvill met in Newcastle, in the north of England, in 1982. They liked to listen to, tell and laugh at stories with their friends. They sent some of these stories to the *Guardian* newspaper. The people at the paper liked them too, and put them in the newspaper every week.

In 1991 they put the best of their stories in a book – *Urban Myths*. More books of stories followed the first, and they talked about their books on BBC television and radio.

They live in London. Phil teaches at a university. Rick is a writer.

Chapter 1   That's Life

No Jobs in the Cupboard

Billy, a young man from London, had no job. He lived with his mother, Mrs Harris. One day he asked her, 'How can I get a job?'

'Look in the newspaper,' she answered. So he bought a paper and looked for jobs.

There were a lot of jobs in London. He read the paper from front to back but most of them were not right for him. Suddenly he saw a good job in an office so he wrote a letter to the boss of the office and sent it. A week later he got a letter from the boss, Mr Davidson. He showed the letter to his mother: 'Please come to my office next Monday. I want to meet you and we can talk about the job.' Mrs Harris was quite excited and Billy was happy – but he was also very nervous.

On the Monday morning Billy got up early and had breakfast. He left the house and went to Mr Davidson's office. There were seven people there for one job. Mr Davidson asked him to come into his office and the other six people waited outside. He asked Billy a lot of questions – he was nervous and he answered the questions badly. When Mr Davidson finished he smiled at Billy and said, 'Thank you, Mr Harris. Please wait outside.'

Billy thought, 'I didn't answer all those questions very well.' He stood up and walked to the door . . . but he made a mistake. It wasn't the door out of the office – it was a cupboard!

'What can I do now? Do I stay in the cupboard and wait or do I go back into the office?' he thought. 'Perhaps I'll stay here and wait. When they're all gone I can come out again.'

Mr Davidson spoke to the other six people and one by one they went out. At five o'clock Mr Davidson went home. Billy didn't know the time so he stayed in the cupboard. He was very tired and he went to sleep. He slept for a long time.

Next morning the cleaner came in. She opened the door of the cupboard and found Billy.

'What are you doing here?' she asked.

'I came here for a job. Did I get it, do you know?'

The Wrong Lover

A man from London, Mr Harvey, had a very beautiful young wife. He was much older than his wife and he began to think she was in love with a younger man. For many weeks he thought about his wife and this other man. Every day he went to work and he was more and more unhappy when he thought about them together.

'What can I do? Am I too old for her? Perhaps she doesn't love me,' he thought. He knew that his wife was at home all day. 'What does she do? Is she happy? Does she meet other men?'

One day Mr Harvey thought, 'I'll go home in the afternoon. I don't usually arrive home at this time so perhaps I can catch my wife with her young man.' He arrived at his house at 2.30 that afternoon and he was very angry because there was an expensive red car in front of his house.

'That's the young man's car,' he thought. He sat in his car and made a plan. 'I know, I'll break the windows of the car!' He found a small heavy box in his car and he broke every window of the red car with it . . . and the lights. After that he sat and waited.

Five minutes later a young man came out of Mr Harvey's house and said goodbye to the beautiful Mrs Harvey. Then this young man walked across to a big tree in the front garden, took an old bicycle and rode away down the street.

'What are you doing here?' the cleaner asked.

The Bigger, the Better?

A rich woman drove her big expensive new car to the supermarket. She arrived and thought, 'There aren't many places to park the car ... where can I leave it?' Suddenly she saw a parking place between a big blue car and a motorbike but it was very small. 'It's going to be very difficult to get this big car in there, but I'll try.'

At the same time two young women in a small old car came to the supermarket. 'Where can we put the car?' the driver asked her friend.

'Look, there's a good place ... near that blue car over there,' she said. It was the same parking place between the blue car and the motorbike.

'Oh, yes,' the driver said. 'I can easily get in there.'

The rich woman started to turn her car into the parking place. 'I hope I *can* get in there,' she thought.

Suddenly the two young women drove into the parking place in front of her. The driver opened the window, looked at the rich woman and said, 'When you learn to drive that big car, then you can do that, too!'

The rich woman was very angry but she said nothing. She turned her car and drove back as far as she could. Then she drove fast at the small car and hit it hard. She broke the lights and other things on the small car. She opened her window and called to the two young women, 'When you have money, then you can do that, too!'

The rich woman drove fast at the small car and hit it hard.

Cheap and Easy

In a small town in the north of England there was a big library with a lot of interesting books in it. People in the town could take the books home for four weeks and read them. They could have as many as four books each time – different books about animals, boats, cooking and holidays or love stories, and then they had to take them back to the library.

Every year the library bought more and more books and soon the building was too small for all the books. One morning in early autumn the boss said, 'November 28th is a big day for us – we're going to move to a new library building. It's a much bigger and better building but there's one difficult problem . . . it's going to be very expensive to move all our books to the new building. Where are we going to find the money and the time?' the boss asked.

The people in the library thought about this problem. One evening five weeks before November 28th a young woman thought of a good plan. She went and talked to the boss about it. He was very interested and together they planned it all carefully. Two weeks later the boss told the people about the plan: ' Between now and November 28th everybody can take six books home, not four books as usual . . . and they can have the books for six weeks, not four.'

Everybody in the town was very happy and they took five or six books home. After two weeks most of the books were out of the library. On November 28th the big day arrived and they moved to the new building. It was quite easy because they had only a small number of books to move there. In the month after the move everybody took their books to the new library. The boss was very happy because it was quite cheap to move and it was quick and easy, too.

In an important game of golf Willie Fraser, one of the best players, had a bad day. First he hit the ball into the trees, then he made a mistake and his ball hit another player, after that he hit the ball badly every time. 'This isn't too good – I must be more careful,' he thought. The first half of the game went badly. He lost five balls.

A friend watched him and said, 'Perhaps you'll have better luck in the second half.'

'Wait and see,' Willie answered. He wanted to play well for this important game but everything went wrong in the second half, too! He lost more balls, he hit more trees, and then he hit the ball near a river. He walked up to the ball and hit it again.

Everybody stopped to watch the ball. 'Will it go into the water? Perhaps he'll be lucky.'

But Willie wasn't lucky – his ball went into the water. He took his golf bag and threw it into the river after the ball. 'Never again! That's it! I'm finished with golf!' And he walked away angrily to his car.

Suddenly he stopped, turned and walked back to the river. All the players stopped again and waited. Willie arrived at the river and walked very slowly into the water. He stopped and carefully put his head under the water.

'Oh no,' his friend thought. 'This is dangerous – I must help him!' The friend ran to the river and was ready to jump into the water after Willie, when suddenly Willie found his golf bag, opened it, pulled out the keys of his car, climbed out of the river and walked away.

'That's strange – it's a Liverpool bus ticket . . . from 1930!'

Hit and Hear

Charlie, a man about 75 years old, often went to a bar in London and met his friends for a drink. He liked a beer or two and he also liked to talk and laugh. In the bar he and his friends remembered the old days and told stories about when they were young.

Charlie had one big problem: he couldn't hear anything in his left ear. When his friends spoke to him they had to sit on his right. He couldn't hear anything because of an accident – he was quite young at the time. One day in 1930, when he was a small boy, he was on a bus in Liverpool with his mother. The bus hit a car and young Charlie hit his head on the floor. From that day he could only hear in his right ear.

One evening Charlie was with his friends, Bert and Jack, in the London bar and Bert told a good story about the old days. Charlie liked the story very much and began to laugh. He laughed and laughed and fell off his chair. He hit his head on the table and something fell out of his left ear, on to the table. Bert took a small white thing from the table and said, 'What's this? I think it came out of your ear.'

Jack looked at the white thing and answered, 'It's a bus ticket.' He looked again and said, 'That's strange – it's a Liverpool bus ticket . . . from 1930!'

Suddenly Charlie said, 'Oh, listen! I can hear in my left ear!'

'What?' said Jack. 'I don't understand . . .'

'I couldn't hear with my left ear because that bus ticket was in my ear all that time!' answered Charlie. They all laughed about the 1930 Liverpool bus ticket. And now his friends can sit on his right *or* on his left in the bar.

In a new factory outside town the people in the office didn't like Mr Taylor, their boss.

One day at lunch-time Mr Taylor walked through a market near his office. He saw some hats and thought, 'I like those brown and black hats – very nice!' He thought about the hats for two or three minutes. 'Perhaps I'll buy a brown hat tomorrow. I can wear it to work.'

The next day he went back to the market and bought a brown hat. He wore it to work every day after that. But Mr Taylor's brown hat was more for the garden than for the office, so everybody in the office laughed at him about it behind his back.

Two weeks later, two of the men from the office were in the market and they saw some hats. 'Look at those hats! They're the same as the boss's new hat,' one man said.

'That's right . . . he's got a brown one,' the other man answered. 'Let's buy the same hat . . . no, *two* hats! I've got a plan. Listen . . .'

The men bought two more hats the same colour as Mr Taylor's hat, but one hat was much bigger and the other was much smaller.

The next day, when Mr Taylor was out for his lunch, the two men took his hat and left the bigger hat in the same place. At the end of the day he took his hat and put it on. 'This hat's too big!' he thought. 'Why? I don't understand.'

The next day, when Mr Taylor was in the factory, the two men took the bigger hat and left the smaller hat in its place. When he was ready to go home Mr Taylor put on this hat but it was very difficult. 'Something's wrong here,' he thought. 'This hat's too small. But I *think* it's my hat.'

On some days Mr Taylor's hat was too big, on other days it was too small and on some days it was right. After two weeks of these problems with his hat Mr Taylor began to think that something was wrong with his head so he went to a doctor. 'I've got a very

'Something's wrong here,' Mr Taylor thought.
'This hat's too small. But I think *it's* my hat.'

unusual problem, doctor,' he said. 'My head is bigger one day and smaller the next . . . and sometimes it's OK. What do you think is wrong with me?'

Red Faces at Christmas

Mr and Mrs MacDonald lived in a small town in Scotland with their three sons. One morning in November they got a letter from Mrs MacDonald's brother, Tom King, and his wife Susan, in London. Mrs MacDonald read it to her husband:

Please come and have Christmas with us in our new house. It's very big so you can all stay here. Come on December 24th. We're going out that evening and we'll be home late, after midnight, but you'll find the key for the front door in a small box behind the tree on the right of the garage door. We'll see you then.

'That's nice,' Mr MacDonald said. 'It'll be interesting to see their new house.' The three boys were excited because they liked London.

On December 24th the MacDonald family drove down to London. They arrived there late that evening and found the right street and the new house. There were no lights in the street so it was very dark. Mr MacDonald parked the car in front of number 22 and they all got out. 'Right!' he said. 'First, let's find the key.'

Mrs MacDonald said to the boys, 'Go and look for the key in the box behind the tree . . . it's on the right of the garage door.'

The boys came back after two or three minutes. 'We can't find the key. We looked carefully but it isn't there,' the oldest boy said.

'What do we do now?' Mrs MacDonald asked. 'There are no lights in the house.'

'Remember Tom's letter — they'll be home very late this evening . . . after midnight,' Mr McDonald said. 'Perhaps the front door is open ... let's see.' They were lucky – the front door was open. They went in and turned on the lights. They went through to the kitchen – everything was new. Mrs MacDonald made some tea and they sat in the front room and drank it.

Mr MacDonald looked at some photographs on the desk. He turned to his wife and said, 'I don't know any of the people in these photos. Do you?'

Mrs MacDonald looked at them and answered, 'No, it's not my brother and his family ... perhaps they're photos of their friends.'

They finished their tea and went up to the bedrooms. They were tired after the long drive from Scotland so they all slept well.

They went through to the kitchen – everything was new.
Mrs MacDonald made some tea.

The next day was Christmas and the MacDonald family came down for breakfast. They went into the kitchen and saw a man and a woman there – but they didn't know them!

'Who are you?' asked Mr MacDonald.

'Philip and Rosemary Brown. This is our house. Who are you?'

'Oh, no! This isn't Tom King's house?' Mrs MacDonald said. 'I'm Janet MacDonald, Tom's sister. He asked us to stay for Christmas. We arrived late last night and couldn't find the key, but the door was open so we walked in.'

Mr and Mrs Brown laughed. 'This is number 22 – Tom lives at number 20. These houses are all new – and they're all the same.'

With red faces the MacDonald family went next door to number 20. 'Happy Christmas,' Mr Brown said, 'and come back and see us some time.'

Where Did I Leave My Wife?

Stan Graham drove quickly along the road one night. His wife, Maggie, slept next to him. Usually Stan and Maggie talked together in the car so he didn't go to sleep. This time she was very tired so she slept. After driving for about 150 kilometres Stan was tired. 'I must find a restaurant . . . I want a cup of coffee and some food,' he thought. There were a lot of restaurants along the road so he stopped and bought something to eat.

When he went back to the car he turned on the radio and drove along for another 50 kilometres. Then he asked his wife, 'Maggie, do you want a cup of coffee?' No answer. He asked again, 'Do you want some coffee, Maggie?' Again no answer. Then he turned to her – but she wasn't there!

He stopped the car and looked in the back – no Maggie!

'Oh, no!' he thought. 'Perhaps she went into that restaurant after me and I didn't see her.' He started to think about the

Maggie was very tired so she slept. After driving for about 150 kilometres Stan was tired.

restaurant but he was very tired. 'This is not very easy. I drove past a lot of different restaurants. Which restaurant was it? I can't remember!'

The Taxi Driver, the Germans and the Plan

Harry, a friendly taxi driver, was in his car outside Waterloo Station in London. It was a quiet day in spring and not many people wanted a taxi. Suddenly he saw two women with a book. They looked at it but he could see that they didn't understand. The two women walked over to Harry's taxi and spoke to him.

'Do you speak German?' one of them asked in German. Harry couldn't speak German but he smiled, opened the door of his taxi and pushed them inside with their bags. 'These German visitors want to see the famous places of London,' he thought. 'I'll drive them round the city and show them everything and they'll pay me a lot of money!'

The two visitors said a lot of things to him in German but Harry didn't understand them. He drove to Buckingham Palace, Big Ben, St Paul's Cathedral and many other interesting places. But the women didn't look happy. 'I think they're angry,' Harry thought. 'I can't understand it, I showed them a lot of famous places but they're angry.' Then he drove to the Tower of London and stopped the taxi. There were a lot of visitors outside the Tower so Harry got out of his car. He asked two or three people, 'Do you speak German?'

One girl said in English, 'Yes, I do'.

'Can you please help me?' he asked. 'Can you ask these German women in my taxi about their problem?'

The girl spoke to the visitors in German. Then she smiled and said, 'Did you take them from Waterloo Station, round the centre of London and then to the Tower?'

'Yes, that's right,' said Harry.

'Did they have a book in their hands at the station?' she asked.

'Yes, they did,' he said. 'It was a guidebook, I think.'

'No, it wasn't!' she laughed. 'It was a British Rail book with plans of all the train stations in London – they only wanted to find the restaurant at Waterloo Station!'

Chapter 2   Accidents

Falling into Bed

Last autumn an Englishman went to the United States for a month and visited all the important places in his guidebook. In the fourth week he went to New York for three days and on the last day of his holiday he looked in the guidebook for the last time. 'Oh, I must visit the Empire State Building . . . it's famous. I'll go up to the top floor – you can see all the city from there . . . that'll be good!'

The weather was cold and it was very windy but he walked up . . . and up . . . and up. He arrived at the top and looked down at the street below – the cars and people were very small.

Suddenly there was a strong wind and he fell off the building. The people in the street stopped and watched . . . he fell fast. But when he was only a hundred metres from the street, a big car came round the corner with a bed on top of it. He hit the bed, not the road. Lucky man!

The Flying Cow

One afternoon a famous television news-reader drove very fast in his open-topped car along a big road. Suddenly there was a strange noise . . . THUD! 'What's that?' he thought. He stopped, turned round and looked – there was a cow in the back! It was dead.

'I must get it out of here,' he thought. 'A dead cow isn't good for my nice clean car.' But the cow was very heavy and he couldn't move it.

So he drove to the nearest town and looked for a garage. He wanted the people in the garage to help with moving the cow. But before he arrived at the garage he stopped at a bar for a drink. When he went into the bar the people said, 'Oh look, it's the famous news-reader on TV. Why is he here?' Then he told them about the cow from the sky.

'Never! It can't be! Is it a story for TV?' the man behind the bar asked.

'No, it happened only twenty minutes ago,' the news-reader said.

A man in the corner of the bar started to laugh. 'Twenty minutes ago I drove across a bridge over the big road,' he said. ' There were some cows in the road . . . I hit a very big cow. It fell off the bridge on to the road below. I stopped and looked for it but I couldn't find it. Now I know: it fell into your car and you drove away with it!'

Look Before You Jump

Some years ago Peter, a young man from a small town, wanted a motorbike. At Christmas he asked for a motorbike but no luck. He finished school in July and hoped for a motorbike then, but no luck. For his birthday in September he asked again – and at last he was lucky! Peter's father gave him a big red motorbike and he was very, very happy.

On his birthday, his father said, 'You must have some lessons, Peter. You must learn to ride the motorbike well.'

'I jumped out in front of the wrong motorbike!'
Mr Fletcher said.

Peter had a very good teacher, Mr Fletcher, and he was a fast learner. Mr Fletcher was happy with his student and one day they stood on the street in the centre of town. 'Today you must learn to stop quickly. Please ride out of town and then come back along this street. I'll suddenly jump out in front of you and say

'Stop!' Stop as quickly as you can. Do you understand?'

'Er . . . yes, I do,' Peter answered. Then he rode away down the street. Ten minutes later he came back round the corner into the same street. He looked for Mr Fletcher but couldn't see him.

'That's strange,' he thought. 'When is he going to jump out and say "Stop!"?'

He rode along and watched carefully but Mr Fletcher wasn't there. Then Peter saw a man on the street under a big red motorbike – a young man stood by him. Peter stopped, parked his bike and ran over. 'Oh, no!' he said. 'That's Mr Fletcher!' He turned to the two men and asked, 'What happened?'

Mr Fletcher slowly sat up and answered, 'I jumped out in front of the wrong motorbike!'

Don't Lose Your Teeth

Some old men, all of them more than 75 years old, went fishing in their boat one sunny morning. At first the sea was quiet and they caught fish easily – each of them got four or five small fish. They talked and laughed a lot and remembered the old days.

Suddenly Bill looked at the sky and said, 'It's quite dark over there.' They all looked up at the sky. 'And there's a strong wind now . . . we must be careful.' The sea was dark, too, and the boat moved up and down in the wind. They stopped fishing and turned on the radio so they could hear about the weather – it was bad news.

The wind was stronger and stronger and the boat moved more

'Hey, look! Here are your teeth, Bill – this fish
swallowed them.'

and more. The men stopped talking and watched the sky. Then Bill was ill and lost his breakfast into the water – and his false teeth went in, too! 'Oh, no!' he said. 'My teeth went into the water too! What can I do?'

'Bad luck! But you can't do much about it,' his friend, Fred, answered. 'Perhaps a fish will swallow them.' And he laughed.

Later, when the sea was quieter, the men started fishing again. After ten minutes Fred caught a very big fish. 'Look at this!' he said to his friends. 'It's quite heavy – six kilos or more.' He cut the fish open, took out *his* false teeth and put them inside the fish.

Then Fred gave the fish to Bill and said, 'Hey, look! Here are your teeth, Bill – this fish swallowed them.'

Bill took the teeth out of the fish and put them into his mouth. Then he took them out again, smiled at Fred and said, 'No, they aren't my teeth – they're too big.' And he threw the teeth into the sea.

Never Leave Your Name

One Saturday afternoon an old woman, Mrs Roberts, sat in the park in the centre of town and talked to her friend, Mrs Jones. They watched the people and talked about life in the town.

There were a lot of cars on the road and one young man parked his new red car near the two women and went off to the shops. After five minutes a big black taxi came fast round the corner of the street and – CRASH! – it hit the red car.

'Oh, no! Look at that young man's car!' Mrs Roberts said to her friend.

'Yes, it's not too good,' Mrs Jones answered.

The taxi driver stopped and got out. He looked carefully at the red car and thought: 'I'll leave a letter on the front

22

'Everybody thinks my name is on this paper but it isn't!' they read.

window ... now, let me think ...' Then he looked round and saw the two women in the park.

He walked across to them and asked for some paper and a pen. 'I want to write a letter about the accident and leave my name and phone number,' he said. He then wrote something on the paper and left it on the front window of the red car. After that he got into his taxi and drove away.

Ten minutes later the driver of the red car came back from the shops. He looked at his car and was very angry. Then he took the letter, read it and got angrier.

Mrs Roberts walked over to him. 'What's the problem?' she asked. 'I saw the taxi driver – he wrote his name and phone number on the paper.'

So the angry young man showed her the taxi driver's letter. It said: 'Everybody thinks my name is on this paper but it isn't!'

Chapter 3   Doing Wrong

Hit the Floor!

Jenny and Robert Slater were on holiday in America. They were young and it was their first time away from home in England. They had a car and visited many famous and interesting places.

'I want to see New York,' Jenny said one morning. 'Let's go there.'

'Mmm, I don't know, love. Everybody says New York's a dangerous place and there are a lot of very strange people there,' her husband answered.

'We'll be careful,' said Jenny. 'Then we won't have any problems.'

So they arrived in New York early in the evening and found a hotel. Later they went out and drove round the streets. They didn't have any problems. 'See,' Jenny said. 'Nothing to be afraid of.'

They had dinner in a good restaurant and then went to a cinema. They arrived back at their hotel at midnight. Under the hotel was a garage so they drove into it and left the car. It was quite dark there and they couldn't see very well.

'Where's the lift?' Jenny asked.

'Over there, I think, near the door,' Robert answered. 'Come on, let's go. I don't like this dark place.'

Suddenly they saw a very tall young man with a big black dog. They were nervous and walked past him as fast as they could to the lift. The door of the lift opened and Jenny and Robert got in. Before the doors closed the man and the dog jumped in – three people and one big black dog in the lift.

'On the floor, Girl!' the tall man said. Jenny and Robert were afraid now, so they quickly got down on the floor. When the lift stopped at the next floor, they stood up, gave the man all their money and got out fast.

'On the floor, Girl!' the tall man said. Jenny and Robert quickly got down on the floor.

'That man was a robber! Perhaps he had a gun ... It's dangerous here!' Robert said. 'We're going to leave New York *now*!'

'Yes, you're right.' Jenny answered. 'There *are* some dangerous people in New York.'

First thing next morning they took their room key to the desk and gave it to the woman. 'There's nothing to pay, Mr Slater,' she said. 'A tall young man with a nice dog came to the desk late last night and paid for your room. Oh, wait a minute – he left this for you, too.' She gave Robert an envelope.

He opened it carefully and took out a letter. They read it together: 'Here's your money and I'm very sorry you were afraid in the lift last night. "Girl" is the name of my dog.'

Joe is a very lucky man – he loves motorbikes and he loves his job. He's lucky because he rides a motorbike in his job in London. He takes letters and important papers from one office to another. There are a lot of cars and buses in London but Joe can ride quickly from one place to the next on his motorbike.

One morning a man telephoned Joe and said, 'Please come to my office *now*!' Joe rode as fast as he could – it took only about ten minutes to get there. He ran up to the office on the fourth floor.

The man gave him a small envelope and a big bag. 'Take this envelope and the bag to the National Bank on Oxford Street and give them to the cashier. Then bring the bag back to my office as soon as possible. Go on – quickly!' he said.

Joe left the office and rode to the National Bank. He parked his motorbike outside the bank and went in. He gave the man's bag and the envelope to one of the cashiers. The woman opened the envelope and read the letter – she looked carefully at Joe and read it again.

'Please wait a minute,' she said. 'I must talk to my boss.' The cashier went away and Joe waited.

Five minutes later a lot of policemen ran into the bank. 'That's him!' one of the policemen said. They took Joe by his arms and pushed him into the police car.

'What did I do?' he asked. 'What's happening?' The policemen didn't answer.

Later at the police station one of the men gave the letter to Joe. 'Here – look at this!' he said. Joe took the letter and read it slowly: 'Put all your money in the bag. I have a gun and I'll use it.'

Late one night Harry Green was in his car in east London. He wanted to get home quickly. He remembered his wife's words that morning: 'Be careful in east London, Harry. There was a story in the newspaper about a dangerous man out there – the police want to catch him. He killed some people with a knife last month ... in east London.'

There was heavy rain that night so Harry didn't drive fast. Suddenly he saw an old woman at the bus stop. 'She'll get wet in all this rain,' he thought. So he stopped the car, opened the window and spoke to the woman: 'Do you want me to take you somewhere? You'll get very wet there at the bus-stop.'

'Mmm,' she answered and got into the car. Harry talked to the old woman and asked her a lot of questions but she only said ' Mmm'. Then he looked at her more carefully. She had a big bag in her hands – it was old and dirty.

'She's got big strong hands ... and a lot of black hair on the back of her hands. That's very strange,' he thought.

Harry started to think: those big hands, all that hair on them ... and then he remembered his wife's words that morning. 'What can I do?' he thought. 'I must get her out of the car ... and that big bag.'

Harry turned to the woman and said, 'I think I've got a problem with the lights at the back of the car.' He stopped the car and asked, 'Can you get out and look at them for me? I don't think they're working.'

The old woman got out and walked round to the back of the car. She left her bag in the car next to Harry. He quickly shut the door and drove to the nearest police station. He took the bag in with him – it was quite heavy, too heavy for an old woman. A policeman took him into a small room and Harry told him the story of the old woman with the hair on her hands.

'What can I do?' Harry thought. 'I must get her out of the car . . . and that big bag.'

The policeman took the bag, opened it carefully and looked inside. 'I think you were very lucky, sir,' he said. 'Look at this!' And he showed Harry a long heavy knife.

Hats On!

When all the good people are in bed at night the police go round the streets and watch the banks and shops and other buildings. One night after midnight Trevor Taylor, a young policeman, was in the street in the centre of town when he saw that one small shop had its door open. He looked through the door and he could see a lot of books, newspapers and cigarettes.

'Perhaps somebody's inside the shop,' he thought, so he slowly pushed the door and walked in. He looked round but found nobody in the shop, so he called the police station on his radio.

Trevor was a heavy smoker and there were a lot of cigarettes in the shop. He quickly took a box of cigarettes and put them under his big policeman's hat. Then he went through to the back of the shop but he didn't find anybody there.

About five minutes later a man came running along the street and arrived at the door. 'This is my shop,' he said, 'and I want to thank you for seeing the open door.' He looked at Trevor and asked, 'Do you smoke?'

'Er . . . yes, I do,' the young policeman answered.

'Good! Here! Take three of these boxes of cigarettes – a small "thank you",' he said.

'No, no, I can't . . . I'm very happy to help you. It's my job,' said Trevor, 'and I haven't a place to put them.'

'That's no problem,' said the man from the shop. 'Put them under your hat!'

'Put them under your hat!'

29

The head of the big bank in the centre of town telephoned the police at about three o'clock one afternoon. 'Come quickly! We had a robber in here – he left only two minutes ago!'

It was very easy to catch this bank robber. When the police arrived at the bank, the cashier told them about the robbery. 'It was all very sudden . . . this man came into the bank and walked over to my window. He pushed an envelope across the desk to me with some words on it: "Give me all the money, I've got a gun".'

'What did you do?' asked the policeman.

'I looked at the envelope for a moment . . . I was quite nervous. Then I gave the robber all the money in my desk . . . it happened very fast. He ran out with the money in a green bag,' she answered. 'Oh, here's his envelope . . .,' and she gave the policeman the robber's envelope.

When the robber left the bank, he went home. It was half-past three. He turned on the radio and listened to the news but there was nothing about the robbery. But half an hour later, when a police car arrived at his house, he knew something was wrong.

'How did you find me?' he asked.

'It was easy,' answered one of the policemen. 'The cashier gave us your envelope – with your name and address on it. So here we are!'

Chapter 4   Living and dying

Dead Cold

In the old Soviet Union (Russia) it was often hard to buy food. Meat was the most difficult thing to find. When people wanted to buy something they usually had to wait in a long line before they could get it and pay for it.

One day in Moscow some years ago, there was the usual long line of people at the cashier's desk in a shop. It was winter and the weather was quite cold. In the line there was an old woman with a very big hat on her head. She waited quietly with the other people, but then suddenly she fell to the floor.

'What's wrong with her?' somebody asked.

'Get a doctor!' another person said.

One man in the line was a doctor so he quickly went over to the woman on the floor. He looked at her carefully and took her hand. Then he took off her hat – under it was a frozen chicken. 'Oh, that's very sad,' the doctor said. 'I think she took the chicken and put it under her hat because she didn't have any money to pay for it.' But the chicken was too cold – she had a frozen head. The chicken killed her.

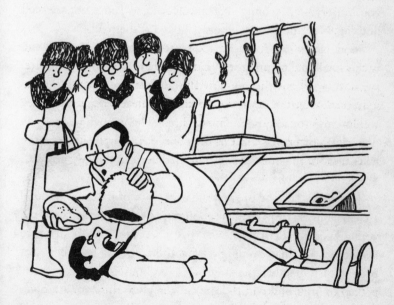

The doctor took off the woman's hat – under it was a frozen chicken.

31

Coat from the Dead

One evening a man called James was on the road from Oxford to London. There weren't many cars on the road because it was late. Suddenly in the lights of his car he saw a woman by the road – she was quite young and very pretty. 'It's dangerous to walk along the road when it's dark and late,' he thought. He stopped, opened the window and asked the young woman, 'Where are you going? It's dangerous to stand here at night . . . perhaps I can take you to London with me.' The young woman didn't answer but she opened the door of the car and got in.

James asked here a lot of questions: 'What's your name? Where do you live? Why are you on the road at night? Is your family in London? Where are your friends? Have you got any money? Are you hungry?' The young woman sat next to James but she said nothing. Not one word. She only looked at the road.

Soon James stopped asking questions and they drove along without talking. Coming into London there were more cars and James had to drive more slowly. Suddenly the young woman started to open the door so James stopped the car quickly. They were in front of a house on a long street. The woman opened the door and got out of the car, then she slowly walked up to the front door of the house. James watched her and thought angrily, ' She didn't say "Thank you".'

Three days later he opened the back door of his car and found a coat. 'This isn't my coat,' he thought. Then he remembered the young woman. Perhaps it was her coat. He had to drive to London again that evening so he thought, 'I'll take her coat back . . . I remember the street and the house.' He drove there, parked in front of the house and walked up to the door. An older woman answered.

'Does a young woman live here?' he asked. 'I think this is her coat – she left it in my car three days ago.'

The woman looked at the coat and began to cry. 'That was my daughter's coat . . .'

'Here, please give it back to her then,' James said.

'I can't,' the woman said. 'She's dead.'

'Dead!' said James.

'Yes, she died five years ago.'

'*Five years* ago?' James asked quietly.

'Yes, on the road between Oxford and London . . . in an accident,' the woman said.

Beer Today, Gone Tomorrow

John Buss lived in Manchester with his grandfather, Frank – an old man of 92! But Frank wasn't happy. He was in hospital. He didn't like the noise in the hospital very much and it was too hot, he told John, when he visited his grandfather one afternoon.

'Can I bring you something when I come next time?' John asked. 'I can visit you again tomorrow.'

His grandfather answered quickly. 'Oh, yes, please . . . bring me some beer,' he said very quietly and looked round carefully. Nobody heard him – only John. 'I usually drink two or three beers every day but they don't give me any in this place.'

'But, Grandad, you can't drink beer in here. You know that – the doctor told you.'

'I know, I know . . . be careful. Put the beer in a bag, then nobody will see it.'

So the next day John went back to the hospital with some bottles of beer in a bag and gave it to his grandfather. The old man looked in the bag, smiled and said, 'Oh, thank you, John. Thank you. Now I'm happy.' Frank opened a bottle and drank it. He opened a second bottle and drank it. After that he opened a third bottle . . .

John laughed because he remembered the bottles of beer.
His grandfather liked beer and was always happy with
a bottle in his hand.

Two days later the doctor telephoned John. 'I'm sorry, Mr Buss, but I have some sad news for you . . . your Grandad died last night. But he was happy – he had a smile on his face.'

John laughed because he remembered the bottles of beer. His grandfather liked beer and he was always happy with a bottle in his hand.

'Did you bring him some beer?' the doctor asked.

'Er . . . yes, I did,' John answered. 'He had two or three bottles two days ago.'

'Oh, I see,' the doctor answered. 'He was happy because he had some beer.'

'But I don't understand,' John thought. 'I took him long life beer!'

ACTIVITIES

Chapter 1

Before you read

1 A *myth* is a strange story. An *urban* myth happens in a town or city. Perhaps it happened – perhaps it didn't. Can you think of any myths from your country?

2 Find these words in your dictionary.

   beer golf guidebook key library
   motorbike nervous park ride

   Which of these words can you

   a read?   **d** feel?   **g** go into?
   b drink?   **e** play?   **h** open a door with?
   c do with a car?   **f** travel on?

After you read

3 What are these people's mistakes, and what happens to them because of their mistakes?

   a Willie Fraser   **b** Mr Taylor   **c** the MacDonalds

4 Which of these people are or will be angry at the end of the story? Who will they be angry with, and why?

   a Mr Davidson   **e** Mr and Mrs Brown
   b the person with the expensive red car   **f** Maggie Graham
   c the two women in the small old car   **g** the Germans
   d Mr Taylor

5 Which stories are these sentences about? Who would say them?

   a He didn't say it was the wrong door.
   b He didn't look in the car first.
   c Her idea about the books was very good.
   d He didn't see a doctor for 70 years.
   e Why don't they learn some English?

6 Work with another student. Have this conversation between Mr Harvey and the person with the expensive red car.

   Student A: You are Mr Harvey. You are very sorry about the car. You don't want the other person to call the police. Don't tell him about your wife or her boyfriend.

37

Student B: You are the person with the red car. You are very angry. You are not happy with Mr Harvey's answers to your questions. You want to call the police.

Chapter 2

Before you read

7 Find these words in your dictionary:

cow   false   swallow

Put the words into these sentences.

a We get milk from a ......

b He lost his teeth in an accident. Now he has ..... teeth.

c She fell into the river and ..... a lot of water.

8 What was your worst accident? What happened? How did you feel after the accident? Did it change your life in any way?

After you read

9 Do these people feel happy or unhappy at the end of the story? Why?

a the Englishman in New York

b the TV news-reader

c Mr Fletcher

d Fred

e the driver of the red car

10 You see these people at a party:

Bill   the taxi driver   the news-reader   the Englishman

Who do you want to talk to most? Why? What questions do you want to ask?

Chapters 3–4

Before you read

11 Find these words in your dictionary.

cashier frozen lift robber

Use all of these words in *two* sentences.

12 Some of these stories are about dangerous places. What is the most dangerous place in your city? Why is it dangerous?

After you read

13 Which stories are these sentences about? Who would say them?

   a He didn't want to hurt us.

   b The man in the office is a robber, not me.

   c She had a knife in her bag.

   d Why didn't she say anything?

   e She didn't want to take her hat off.

14 Find the second half of each of these sentences.

a	The man with the dog	likes drinking.
b	Joe	gets into a lift.
c	The woman in Russia	is a heavy smoker.
d	Trevor Taylor	died five years ago.
e	The pretty young woman	doesn't pay for the food.
f	The dangerous killer	loves motorbikes.
g	John's grandfather	has hairy hands.

Writing

15 You are Robert and Jenny Slater. Write a short letter to the man with the dog. Say sorry to him and thank him for his kindness.

16 You are the Englishman in New York. Write a postcard to your friends about your holiday. Tell them about your accident.

17 Finish the story 'Where Did I Leave My Wife?' Does Stan Graham find his wife? Where does he find her? How does she feel? What does she say to him?

18 Write a story for a student magazine. The name of the story is 'Something Strange Happened to Me'.